Praise for *Evaporation*

Evaporation is a gift. Claire Hsu Accomando writes with wonder, precision, and cinematic wisdom. The remembrances and stories of China, France, and America are rendered with tenderness, intelligence, and joy. What a remarkable life there is inside this book, the poet's expansive heart.
—Lee Herrick, California Poet Laureate

Evaporation is a radiant narrative, told in inventive forms. The winds of time, nature, and memory move in this meditation on what endures after loss, what rises from silence, and what carries forward. Claire Hsu Accomando's delicate brushstrokes of language say what we can know before we know. The poems captivatingly hold the sacredness of memory as they point us toward what lasts. This is a remarkable study of language, identity, migration, relation, loss, and how we continue on.
—Janelle Adsit, author of *Unremitting Entrance*

In *Evaporation*, Claire Hsu Accomando's luminous poetic memoir, she shows us the world shaped by wind. People, like flower petals, and scents, are wind-borne: relocated, dislocated, and exiled by war, as well as by the work of peace-making and the human search for stability. Voluptuous with colors and textures, this book of family memory is a vivid gift to the reader that celebrates lived experience recounted with precision before it can slip from our grasp like vapor.
—Barbara Brinson Curiel, author of *Mexican Jenny and Other Poems*

In *Evaporation,* Claire Hsu Accomando pushes at what the memoir can be across forms: prose, poetry, the new archival document, and photography. The choices she deftly makes serve to propel the work, carrying us through observations of beloved kin as well as the distant and yet ever close presence of evil on their lives across place and time. How they persist and resist is always through love: the love of a name written on a note pinned to the bundle of an abandoned child, the love in a distant grave that remains unvisited physically and yet ever tended in the heart and mind, the love of committing to sharing a life towards a common destination. How *we* must persist and resist is through love. Accomando teaches us about the lightness, the belief, and the discipline of love, despite every obstacle. Her consistent and revelatory craft demonstrates a diminutive genius as she balances the narrative's veracity with the minute, other-worldly attention of the poet. In these times of upheaval and tumult, we need this exemplar. I will be teaching this book for decades.
—Raina J. León, author of *black god mother this body*

As editor of *Atlanta Review*, it was my great privilege to publish spectacular poems like "Evaporation" and "Wild Goose Pagoda" by Claire Hsu Accomando. This book lets us enter the extraordinary life, lived in three very different worlds, of the poet behind these profound and heartwarming poems.
—**Dan Veach, author of *Elephant Water* and *Lunchboxes***

Claire Hsu Accomando's autobiographical collection embodies landscapes of love and legacy, awake to the winds of personal and global history that circle and shape the course of her and her family's journey, spanning continents and cultures, including roots in China, France, and America—across decades of war and peace keeping, displacement and connection.

 With a historian's eye and a poet's ear—and especially attuned to a child's fresh observations and depth of wonder—Accomando immerses us in life's vivid, lyrical particulars, including the humorous surprises, spiritual resonances, romantic serendipity, as well as heartbreaks that can ache through lifetimes.

 Spending time with these poems is the pleasure of getting to know a long, vibrant life deeply lived—including the ways our parents', siblings', and children's stories reverberate with our own.
—**Sierra Nelson, author of *The Lachrymose Report***

Evaporation is a collection of poems attentive to life, grounded in place, carved in muscular, precise language. Accomando's work sings within memory and a poet's profound connection to the world.
—**Heather Eudy, author of *Bills of Lading***

Copyedting by Aaron Laughlin
Typesetting by Noelle Doblado
Cover by Sarah Godlin
Cover photo by David Berman

ISBN: 978-1-962081-20-7

First Edition

The Press at Cal Poly Humboldt publishes scholarly, intellectual, and creative works by or in support of our community. The press supports the Cal Poly Humboldt mission to improve the human condition and our environment by promoting understanding of social, economic, and environmental issues.

The Press at Cal Poly Humboldt
1 Harpst Street
Arcata, CA 95521
press.humboldt.edu

EVAPORATION

Claire Hsu Accomando

The Press at Cal Poly Humboldt

CONTENTS

Restless Winds...1
Ab Ovo..2
Whimsical Winds...4

LAND OF DRAGONS

Firecrackers...6
Evaporation...7
Latin Mass..8
Wild Goose Pagoda...9
Girl Child..11
Waiting for Snow Blossom...12
Chinese Papers..14
White Swan Hotel..15
Toothpaste...16
Why Professor Gao Sings...17
Brown and White with Red...19

A POPPY SEED IN AMBER

Paris Morning..22
Sixteen Seasons...23
My Jurassic Village..25
Wartime Cigarette..27
Chartres..28
Premonitions of Death in the Daffodil Month of April......................29
Turkey..34

VIVE LES AMÉRICAINS

My Near Epic Voyage to America...36
America..39
Sharing a House...40
Chicken with Worms..46
Words..49
Flying Lesson...50
Point of View...51
Washington Square to 42nd Street...52
How We Met..54
Before We Met...55
Yankee Colors..56
Winter Pool... 57
Green Van.. 58
Toasting Mama on Valentine's Day... 59
Nine/Eleven Pacific Time... 61
Inheritance..62
The Perfect Death of a Tai Chi Master..63
Black Marker.. 67
Where is My America?...68
Papa's notes on citizenship in an email dated March 29, 1996........... 69
Papa's Rings..71
Wind Advisory..73
Acknowledgements...74
About the Author..76

PHOTO CREDITS

Land of Dragons: photo by David Berman....................................5
Vive Les Américains: photo by Claire Hsu Accomando.................35
Twin Towers: photo by Claire Hsu Accomando............................60
About the Author: photo by Marianne Hsu Santelli.....................76

RESTLESS WINDS

Odysseus's sailors stabbed the leather sack on deck
and let loose the troublesome captive winds.

These wild winds still swirl around the planet,
ignoring barriers, borders, and barricades.

Though invisible, their effects are seen and felt. Wind thumb-
prints are one of a kind. Their footprints leave forensic data.

Some cause evaporation, others form fossils in mudrock.
Master movers—winds transport earthen things from

one place to another using skills that range from
pickpocket agility to gangster brutality.

We are atoms on vapor, suspended
till released. We voyage on restless winds.

AB OVO

Claire
My mother named me
after Claire of Assisi.
At seventeen, I journey
to the luminous hill town
birthplace of my patron saint.

Eight hundred years ago,
young Chiara, not yet a saint,
swapped silk gowns for burlap
tied at the waist with fisherman rope.
A nun, she fed the poor, tended the sick.

I, pilgrim—knapsack on my back—
ascend worn steps to cobbled streets,
strike a match to a white candle
in a red glass, leave trembling poppies
on the ancient floor of the basilica.

Hsu
Fuyun Hsu, my father, left
China at twenty-one. Winner
of a scholarship to study law
in Paris, he came to class
early, sat in the front row

of the amphitheater
opposite the professor
to snatch volleys of French
words he needed to decode
into his native Mandarin.

When he glimpsed a
young woman
afar, standing,
he offered her his seat.
She signaled no,

mortified at the journey
to the pit of the arena. Yet,
not to hurt his feelings, changed
her mind. Thus, Nicolette Laloy
became Mama.

Accomando
My husband's name walked me
to the first row of the alphabet.
Allan took pride in his Italian heritage
until an aging aunt hinted Accomando
masqueraded for Ackerman.

Evading German law,
great-grandpa crossed the Alps
in haste, married a Catholic girl
from Italy, changed his name—
came to America.

Most of the family
denies the story.
Yet, the old man's the only one
buried in a Protestant cemetery,
somewhere back in New Jersey.

Given. Inherited. Acquired.
If I were to change my names,
my origins would remain the same.
Ultimately what matters
in this accident of birth

is where-and-when on earth
whimsical winds
deliver the seeds
that root
our family trees.

WHIMSICAL WINDS

cause tissue blossoms
from peach and plum
to down drizzle
across the slopes of China's
serpentine wall.

From atop minarets,
winds diffuse the call
of muezzins,
also the scent
of roasted sesame.

Air stylists sweep cumuli into pompadours,
tease lacy coifs from feathers
of balding angels, and let the sun
tint their creations pink,
yellow, and brilliant flamingo.

LAND OF DRAGONS

FIRECRACKERS

When Papa was a kid in China, he
watched his older brothers cram gun
powder into narrow cardboard tubes.
They lit fire to string and ran like hell,
little Papa following hands over ears.

Nightfall. Heaven bursting with red chrysanthemums,
shooting stars and blue dogs dancing. Ta-tattat,
ta-tattat. The smell of burnt paper. A scary-head lion.
Under the shimmering cloth—a centipede with
black-cotton slippers on each of its hundred feet.

The golden serpent weaved through narrow streets,
followed by fifteen days of feasting and gambling with
parents and servants. Fifteen days of eating sticky rice
and slow-cooked pork with slippery ivory chopsticks.
Summer in winter. Crimson lanterns in the snow.

EVAPORATION

Pearl-gray Beijing sky.
The sun—a plumb line over the blue-
tiered roof of the Temple of Heaven.

Away from crowds on the worn imperial
path an old man stakes his claim, fills his pail
with water from a plastic bottle.

His brush an artichoke sprouting
from a broomstick. Dipping the tip, he paints
liquid lines on parched pavement—

down stroke on ancient road, upsweep forms
a tail. Top to bottom, sky to earth. He commits
calligraphy to cobblestones.

Two legs walking—a man. Three peaks rising
shape a mountain. Man crossing a mountain
to join another signifies multitudes.

North to south, east to west, watermarks
on fire stones. Summer breezes lift
men, mountains. River words evaporate.

No trace remains on bare rock.
Wearing white cotton gloves
the old man sweeps

dirt,
leaves,
cigarette butts.

Six days a week
a street cleaner.
On Sunday a vapor poet.

LATIN MASS

Standing in line
at Starbucks on Ring
Zhong Road, Beijing.

Years ago, on a Sunday morning
I would have been in church, kneeling—
comforted by the Latin mass.

In Istanbul, Nairobi, Paris or Kabul
with no knowledge of the language
the heavy door pushed open
I was home.

Votive flames in crimson glasses.
Dóminus Vobiscum.
Voices sang back, *Et cum spíritu tuo.*
Now priests speak Turkish, Swahili,
French or Pashto.

No Credo, no Agnus Dei,
to let me know things
are in order in my heart, my head,
the whole mundo.

My turn to order. I point
to a number on a board.
The Chinese woman
in forest green asks,

Caffè?
Latte?
Grande?
Amen, I say. Amen.

WILD GOOSE PAGODA

In Xi'an near the tombs of the terracotta warriors
we're told to be at the Wild Goose Pagoda

at sundown to watch the water show.
It's a tourist magnet. We plan to stay away—

can't hold back. Dusk settles around the old temple
where once, starving monks witnessed the miraculous fall

from heaven of a flock of plump geese.
Tonight, Mozart filters from speakers installed

decades ago to blast Mao's slogans to the masses.
In synchrony with once-banned music, colored lights

like neon gas in glass illuminate columns
of shooting water from holes in warm pavement.

With Vivaldi, jets rise and fall. A visual relief
from the fever heat. Tourists hug the plaza,

flip-flops on their feet. Not the Mexicans in our group of professors.
The women are high-heeled, the men suited in white linen.

Francisco dons a leather vest, Gucci shoes, no less.
The music changes to Tango. Marisol takes Francisco's hand.

They enter the liquid forest at an angle. Toes and knees
leading, shoulders and head tilted back.

With each note, geysers grow taller. The couple appears,
disappears, reappears changing hues in the fluid medium.

Marisol's skirt clings to her legs as flag to flagpole
in the rain. An old man applauds. Girls in cotton frocks rush

into the liquid jungle. As if by divine command, multitudes
follow. Bare-bottom toddlers, young people, aging ones too.

They smile, squeal, slide and glide inside the vertical river
till the music dies. On the way back to the university

in the air-conditioned bus Francisco and Marisol shiver
in their drenched-designer clothes. Laughter escapes

their chattering teeth. Those of us timid and dry
join our wet counterparts. In that cold bus, we know

a purifying moment of exhilaration.
Not unlike the old monks' when, as recorded,

a flock of wild geese landed on the pagoda's tiles—
feathered manna cuffing their narrow ankles.

GIRL CHILD

When the female child is born, the husband allows
his wife to keep her four days, but not to name it.
Mei Lin has an unspoken name for the baby. Had the girl
been firstborn, they might have petitioned for a chance at a boy.

Mei Lin pulls the last stitch on the many-colored quilt.
For nine months she gathered scraps of silk from the textile mill,
sewed together two patchwork squares. Between layers she stuffed
straw, bits of cornhusk. January is cold in Southern China.

Husband and son sleep. Mei Lin warms an empty box
with hot bricks from the oven. She pads the blanket into
the carton that once held fragrant lychee nuts.
The quilt scents of summer fields, a good blend.

Mei Lin lowers the girl in the silk nest, presses her breast
to the baby's sucking mouth for the last time. She tucks
the blanket around the bundle, sews the edges like
an envelope, leaving an opening for the baby's head.

In the husband's shoe she finds a five-Yuan note.
Mei Lin pins bill to quilt, face up.
Money brings attention to itself.
She writes *Snow Blossom* smack on top of Mao's face.

Before folding the flap over the newborn's face
Mother's lips touch the soft cheek—warm as a steamed bao.
The infant stirs. She has not kissed her daughter before.
Nor will she kiss her again.

Certainly not on the steps of the police station
where she'll deliver the carton with its colorful cocoon
and the defaced image of the great leader
looking up toward the black dome of heaven.

Outside, flakes whirl.
A gauze sash girds the horizon.
Dreaded dawn. Mei Lin runs.
Her feet drag like those of an old woman.

WAITING FOR SNOW BLOSSOM

Nanchang, we exit the plane. Icy wind seeps
through the accordion corridor of the jetway.
Rain glistens the tarmac.

Stern airport officials wrapped in greatcoats
shove us along. This is communist China,
not Drunken Master, Jackie Chan's Hong Kong.

My sister Katie and husband Dave
await a daughter, Snow Blossom.
The Internet photo shows a serious child.

Round face, round eyes, round fists protrude
from padded clothes. She's two, wide as she is high.
Red slippers—stitched yellow ducks on toes.

Iris, from Adoption International, buses us
to the Lake View Hotel. The cylinder edifice
rises from a flat, opaque black lake.

We're told to stay in our rooms, be patient.
The children to be delivered one-at-a-time.
Eleven females, one male "with defects."

Snow Blossom travels by train
others by bus. *Hold your emotions,* Iris says
the children have never seen Westerners.

We wait, doors ajar. In the hallway, a baby's cry.
Stampede to the elevator. Doors open.
An attendant hands Danielle a colorful armful.

The single mom came for a toddler. Her
intended baby had a seizure. The People's Republic
crammed a year's red tape into 48 hours.

Danielle will not return alone to Iowa.
She blinks tears
presses baby to heart.

Next. The boy in a black-and-yellow
sweater. Tiny for four.
The cleft palate's not obvious, his limp is.

Parents know about the brain damage.
Even with the double row of happy
buttons, a sad bumble-bee.

Nine more deliveries.
No Snow Blossom.
No message.

Katie and Dave move to the lobby.
Midnight. Trains stop.
Girl comes tomorrow.

Morning—can't decipher the weather.
Winds flat-line the smoke from the city's
kilns. Ash and sky—a shade apart.

Invisible raindrops form concentric
circles as they touch the pewter lake
fifteen floors below my window.

All night, Katie and Dave drink black tea
in tall glasses. We'll meet Snow Blossom
at the Department of Justice.

The cabbie races through red lights, shaves cyclists
in trash-bag rain gear balancing pipes, refrigerators,
piglets in bamboo baskets.

The perilous ride occupies our minds.

No turning back.

CHINESE PAPERS

In rainy Nanchang city—a grainy concrete cube:
the Department of Justice. A metal cage elevates
us to the fourth floor. At the end
of a dark hall a tiny girl stands,
her hair tied in purple rubber bands,
two stiff brushes above her ears.

She's cuter than her photo, my sister
whispers. The toddler and the orphanage
mom have traveled on trains with chickens,
corn and goats. Mrs. Wang coaxes
Snow Blossom forward.
Papa, Mama. Papamama, she urges.

Katie and Dave kneel. The child doesn't move.
Ten little fingers clutch an empty plastic bottle.
Unblinking, she studies the strangers—
refuses their hands.
Mrs. Wang says the baby's name and birth date
were scribbled on a five-Yuan note pinned to her quilt.

She was four days old when found under a duvet
of snowflakes. Born the year of the ox—
a resilient baby. Her windbreaker is new and blue.
Also new, her tennis shoes. She wears four pairs
of pants for warmth, slit at the crotch.
Chinese children wear no diapers.

A paper mountain awaits the parents.
Katie lifts the toddler. The girl pushes her away. In time,
Snow Blossom rests her head on her new mom's shoulder.
In the People's Republic the child must sign with a footprint.
Dave removes the orphanage shoe, peels off the sock.
The official applies red inkpad to foot, presses sole to paper.

Side to side. Back to front.
Katie's name holds up the little piggies.
Dave signs under the heel.
Snow Blossom slumbers through the historic moment.
Year of the Dragon: a propitious year to begin
a journey—a new venture—a family.

WHITE SWAN HOTEL

Final adoption hurdle. The children's passports
are delivered in Guangzhou. We deplane at dusk.
Eleven girls, one boy (with defects).
Two dozen Americans.

From the airport a bumpy ride. Toddlers and infants
stretch their necks. No crying, no smiling. Open eyes.
At every turn, tropical breezes blow through open
windows ruffling their short hair this way and that.

We weave through the narrow streets of Guangzhou,
formerly Canton, where the Opium War began.
Scintillating garlands of light festoon
the bridge over the Pearl River.

On Shamian Island, acres of white limos carpet
the parking lot of the White Swan Hotel.
We roll bags and strollers over antique rugs.
In the lobby a waterfall splashes into a pond

where spotted koi flashpaint red and gold curves
in the water garden. New parents tighten
their grip—worry children might trip on marble
steps, drown in the brocade of fish and lotus.

We don't complain. We celebrate in the dining
room. Orphanage children have giant appetites—
also table manners. No reaching for food. No tears,
no words, no laughter. Buddha faces all around.

Katie and Dave feed their daughter morsels
of tofu at the tip of chopsticks. She picks a grain
of rice from the table, hands it to Dave.
She chews, swallows, shows white teeth for more.

After her third course, Snow Blossom sips soup.
Between the cap of shiny black hair and the rim of white
porcelain, her eyes dart from Dave to Katie. Soup done she
reaches—grabs melon cubes from Mom, pot stickers from Dad.

The stunned parents stare at each other.
The toddler puts down her bowl and
explodes into laughter. Her first sound. Joy
bounces off the walls of the White Swan.

TOOTHPASTE

When the Teacher asks for an example of Regret

Silence. One timid hand rises.
I regret one thing.
Yes, Mei Mei?

Three years ago, when I was five and lived in China
I went to the People's Clinic to get soap, a free gift,
one for each family. All gone, when I arrived.

The nurse gave me a metal tube. Soap for the mouth
she said. Open this cap, give a squeeze on your finger,
rub it on your teeth.

Walking home, the sun opened its oven door on my face. I sat
under the big willow, twisted the cap. A green silkworm crawled
on my finger. I rubbed my front teeth and the ones next to them.

I licked the sweetness with my tongue. Five jelly
ribbons squirted my fingers. The gift from the People's
Clinic ended in my mouth.

When I reached my village, kids sniffed me.
Mei Mei is a bad girl, they told my mother.
She ate the family soap. Go home, children, Mama said.

I showed her the tube thin as wonton dough.
Don't worry Mei Mei.
How could I wash clothes with tooth soap?

I regret I was selfish and ate the soap for the mouth.
The teacher asks: *Is this a good example of regret?*
Thirty-one hands go up in the air.

Mei Mei's eggshell cheeks turn
the color of ripe peach. Her hand
covers the forming of a smile.

WHY PROFESSOR GAO SINGS

On the last day of class in California,
Professor Gao sheds her glasses.

I'll sing in Chinese, my imposed language
then in Mongolian, my native tongue
she tells her students.

The young Americans roll their eyes.
Professor Gao stands—not tall.
First a love song, then a ballad of exile.

Strong, pure, her voice soars over the roar
of campus mowers, through open windows
past red rhododendrons.

A gentle wave of hand symbolizes woman.
A whip slashing the air represents man.
Professor Gao grows tall with high notes.

The students—stunned by the rise of the voice
when the lovers meet, awed by the tones of sorrow
when they part—stop texting under their desks.

The Chinese lovers die.
Silence. Stillness in the classroom.
So sad, the students say.

Professor Gao nods. The next song gouges deep.
More guttural, more Slavic. The melody clears the window,
clears the pink-and-white blossoms of fruit trees in bloom.

Words rise and dip above redwoods—sweep over
pacific waters. Gusty currents nurse the song to Inner
Mongolia where it eagles among high-pile cumuli.

Amidst tall grass, the tune quivers—becomes a sigh.
A young man in Rastafarian locs asks:
Why do you sing, Professor Gao?

I was a child during the Cultural Revolution,
she answers. *Hunger years for a teacher-father*
and a poet-mother. The words Mama wrote

offended Chairman Mao. She must repent.
Of what?
Obscenity, corruption—enemy of the state.

To purify her diseased brain, she must self-criticize.
Her knees hurt. I take her on my bicycle to the People's Square.
Kneeling on hard stones, she retracts lines brushed on thin paper.

Pages shiver, children laugh. She confesses litanies.
We return day   after   day week   after   week
until treason poison is extracted from her mind.

Brain scrubbed, mother still writes.
In elegant words she exalts Mao, composes
hymns of adoration. I uncover her code.

The word idiot burns her head—she bleeds enlightened
on paper. Incomparable proxies for despicable.
I fear saying the wrong thing. I coil in silence.

I become stone. My classmate Peony plays
banned music on her father's secret violin,
Sing, she says.   I remain mute.

After school, we collect wool torn from sheep by barbed wire.
Grass soaks the felt shoes made by our fathers.
Teachers and musicians don't make good cobblers.

Peony catapults her voice past grasslands, past circles of yurts.
She intones a song from Madame Chairman's opera. You know
the words. Sing, she says. I practice in the key of silence,

until my lips part.

My buried-alive voice seeps out, small, timid,
unsure. Words gush forth with the fury
of water held against its will. My voice floods

green plateaus, scattering sheep and yak, carding
plump, wooly clouds. I celebrate that spring day
in Inner Mongolia when I broke silence.

This is why on the last day of school I sing.

BROWN AND WHITE WITH RED

All over, rabbits. I'm Lillian Liu's guide.
This is her third time at the Del Mar Fair.
How can there be so many different rabbits?

she asks. *In China, we have only two kinds—*
brown, and white with red eyes.
That's all.

She stops by a mean-looking, cat-faced, long-
haired rabbit. In her notepad, she writes
the name in English and jots down a vertical version

in Chinese. A 4-H girl cradles two bunnies.
She rocks them like babies. Lillian Liu is riveted.
In China, we can have only one child.

My daughter was born with brain damage.
At thirteen, she cannot feed herself.
My parents care for her while I'm on this

teacher exchange program. Lillian Liu runs
to a double enclosure with a spotted family.
She circles the cage, head tilted to one side.

Chubby rabbits hop back and forth
over the partition. *Two rooms for one family?*
When I married, we lived with my parents.

They had one room. We had the other.
My husband was a chemist, but China needed
farmers in the South. For five years dust

filled his lungs. Despair entered his heart.
An official informed me of his suicide.
A soldier came to partition my room.

Since I no longer have a husband,
he informed me, I am assigned a pensioner.
My daughter and I can share a bed.

But my child wets herself. She needs
her own mattress. The soldier hammered
six more nails into the wall.

I never imagined so many kinds of rabbits,
I'd love to bring my daughter
this black one with hangdown ears. But,

useless animals are not allowed.
We would have to make it into stew,
share with neighbors.

Lillian Liu closes her notebook.
How many varieties of sheep?
she wants to know.

A POPPY SEED IN AMBER

PARIS MORNING

Six thirty. Mariette slips
from the apartment.
I hear her downsteps.
Morning breeze parts lace curtains.

Between brick-red geraniums
on the balcony, I see my cousin
on the street below. Elegant, high-
heeled, younger than her years.

Seven o'clock. The aroma of oven-warm
bread precedes her as she sneaks back,
balancing baguettes and bags
of golden croissants.

My sisters and I dress quickly,
drawn to the table where blue and yellow
bowls of frothy coffee await us. We are
the American cousins, visiting after thirty years.

I, the oldest of four sisters, sleep in Mariette's bed.
Breakfast: sitting on cathedral chairs and a hard futon,
we pull apart the flaky flesh of crispy croissants,
releasing buttery aroma that nourishes the breeze.

In the street, bumpers bang as drivers pivot
their cars inch by inch out of tight spaces.
We sip, cradling bowls with both hands.
Mariette passes the apricot jam.

It's good to have you, she says.
Now that I'm alone,
this place is too big, too silent.
I miss the noises. I miss the voices.

Over refills we plan our day—first Notre Dame
where our parents were married, then the Sorbonne
where they met. We drink slowly. Savor the moment
Capture it like a poppy seed in amber.

SIXTEEN SEASONS

On June 22, 1941, at the start of summer
Hitler bulldozes his tanks into Russia,
bisecting Europe. The Trans-Siberian Railway
is held up in Moscow. Papa, the only civilian
on board, is on his way to China.

We are cut off.

Mama, my brother, and I leave Paris
for my grandparents' ancestral village.
Orange geraniums welcome us.
Nani holds us tight,
Grandpapa doesn't know our names.

Sundays.

We carry baskets with cheese and bread
and walk to the cold river
where Grandpapa swims with glasses
and his corduroy cap.
I pick cherry earrings from the orchard.

No itchy sweaters.

In the fall, with a bee cloud overhead, we push a wheel-
barrow of bruised apples to the cider press in the village hall.
I learn a secret: in the toy closet, Martin the bear needs
to protect a moveable panel where my uncle hides a
radio box. At night, strange voices rise from downstairs.

All is quiet in the morning.

Winter nights. My aunt carries panes of frozen diapers
from the clothesline. She hangs them on a cord in the kitchen.
Mama's knitting needles click like swords as she reads us
stories of brave knights. Nani plays Chopin on the piano.
Baby chicks dance in their crate under the cooling stove.

When water in the pitcher freezes, we don't wash. Too bad.

Spring squeezes the scent of lilac through shutter slats.
Pale yellow daffodils pop from the moist ground,
and we boil onion skins to make red Easter eggs.
The last spring brings eight American soldiers to our
village, they give me five sticks of shooing gum.

Tell me to chew, not swallow.

This is a happy time.
The war is over.
We will reunite with Papa
after four years of separation,
but he will never meet

his second son

the baby who was born
after Hitler cut open Europe,
the toddler who died
before the liberation,
the boy who will never grow

to be a man.

The war is over.
We pretend happiness.
We wave little flags.
Vive la France.
Vive les Américains.

MY JURASSIC VILLAGE

Our house had no number.
No one bothered
with the street name.
Just: Rahon, Jura,
France.

Across the street the baker sold baguettes
and boules straight out of his stone oven.
Burning to the touch, he held each loaf
with doubled-over flour sacks. Big white
handprints marked his black apron.

The smell of warm bread spilled into the
street. Mama cut through the crusty loaf,
impaled oval slices with a fork and held
them over stove fire. Butter melted on our
toasts, forming yellow puddles in the holes.

We needed both hands to bring bread to mouth.
Threads of smoke from burnt edges hovered over
us. War dragged. Flour mixed with sawdust turned
our bread from white to beige to brown. Loaves
grew smaller. The boulangerie closed after lunch.

The oldest, I could use a pointy knife to dig out
mouse droppings that seeded our baguettes.
After Nazi soldiers stole our butter, we used lard.
A sprinkle of salt made our tartines delicious. Dunking
them in coffee from chicory softened the crust.

When a blue-eyed enemy grabbed the egg saved
for my birthday cake, I asked Jesus to break
the thin shell in his leather hand, and let the yolk
run down to his shiny boots. Mama ate
small portions—said she was not hungry.

Wobbly stone steps led to the post office above
the bakery. It also housed the village phone.
When a letter came from China, Madame
la Poste rushed down the stairs in felt slippers
to hand my mother the wrinkled envelope.

Mama   always waiting   met her in the street.

Postmarks from Australia, Switzerland, even
America. Black lines darkened both sides of the
paper. My mother flattened the sheet on the kitchen
table to read Papa's careful cursive letters. He wrote in
French, the language he mastered before my birth.

We drew pictures on thin paper for him.
Heavy letters made planes fall, Mama said.
We told Papa happy things. Not about the Nazis
taking away my aunt and Grandpapa.
Not about Emmanuel sick in his little bed.

Lying on orchard grass, Louis and I
listened to the purring of machines in the sky.
How could a plane fly anyway?
We had twig brooms and galvanized
pails to collect manure balls from the

plough horses as they clopped past our
house on their way to work. A few times a day
Louis and I lowered another bucket down
the well. The chain rattled. After the splash,
we turned the rusty handle to pull the water up.

In winter, our woolen gloves stuck to the handle.
It took both of us to carry the load to the kitchen.
Once we brought up a dead chick.
Once we watched an eclipse
reflected in the dark-circle of water.

We didn't linger at the well,
It was deep. It reached hell.
I've not returned to the village.
I've not seen the grave where
my youngest brother is buried.

The house now has plumbing.
Gardens replace the potato field.
Rahon stands at the foot
of mountains formed
in the Jurassic age.

WARTIME CIGARETTE

Monsieur Emile scoops loose tobacco
from the pocket of his pants. He forms an ant
hill on the table. *Get me the cigarette machine,*
he asks my four-year-old brother, *and roll me one.*

He rips a leaf from his wife's Mass Book. I know
he's gone too far, even for wartime, but I won't tell,
even if my eyes are gouged out under torture.
He tears the page in two, hands Louis one strip.

My brother cradles the paper in the rubber
hammock, sprinkles tobacco crumbs into the groove.
His chubby fingers remove the pocket lint. *Mon
Dieu,* he says, as he gives the handle a turn.

Licking his finger, he slides saliva along the edges,
presses to make the paper stick. Monsieur Emile
holds the lettered tube in his calloused hand.
Perfect, he says. *Shapely as a woman, and juicy too.*

With a piece of straw he steals fire from the stove,
and lights the blasphemy. Flames burn
the word *pacem*, from *Dona nobis pacem*
printed on the transparent liturgical paper.

CHARTRES

Colored fragments of glass pierce the walls
of the cathedral, bedazzling my seven-year-old eyes.
The blues, the red, the purple, spots of
yellow and green. But the blues—the blues.

The kaleidoscopic windows hang tree high.
On the bumpy stone floor my feet step on puddles
of light. Now, my round-toed shoes turn green.
Now red, now yellow and purple and blue.

Children's voices rise, cascading upside—
a reversed waterfall. Wearing gold, the old priest
swings a silver lantern. Incense rises
in luminous arcs above my mystic brain.

PREMONITIONS OF DEATH IN THE
DAFFODIL MONTH OF APRIL

Sweet-scented month of premonitions.
On the fourth we remember Martin Luther King, Jr.
who died in 1968, shot in the jaw by a bullet.
He anticipated death. Many did, in the month of April.
Not my little brother, in France, a long time ago.

April 23, 1616

Shakespeare has a premonition.
A month before his death
he makes his will, disposing
with meticulous care of his material things.
Gives him satisfaction, a sense of accomplishment.
To granddaughter Elizabeth
he bequeaths goods of silver.

One bowl he sets aside for daughter Judith
also £150. The author of *King Lear*
forbids his son-in-law claim to the money.
To friends he leaves his sword
and coins for memorial rings.
He remembers the poor of Stratford.
He adds a postscript—

And to my wife I leave my second best bed.
Crafting documents sets minds at peace.
He's buried near the river Avon, upon
which swans glide and where
on grassy banks daffodils
and weeping willows
grow side by side.

April 15, 1865

Thirteen days prior to his death, Lincoln
has a nightmare. In the dream, he wanders
through the empty White House
silent but for the haunting sounds

of unseen mourners. Entering
the East Room—a coffin
guarded by soldiers. He asks

Who is dead in the White House?
A guard answers, *The President*
he was killed by an assassin.
Abraham Lincoln is shot
on Good Friday,
dies on Holy Saturday
killed by an assassin.

April 12, 1945

Fruit trees bloom
in Warm Springs, Georgia
where Franklin Roosevelt
is recovering.
He's been ill since Yalta.

Worn out from traveling
with atrophied legs, drained
from masking illness for Churchill
and Stalin. FDR has glared at the dark
pupil of death most of his adult life.

Now he rests in an oasis of tranquility
surrounded by family and friends.
Eleanor is not here. Lucy Mercer is—
meeting arranged
by daughter Anna.

While he signs documents
an artist paints his portrait
improving on the ashen flesh tones.
Minutes before
the session ends

Franklin grabs his head.
His last words: *I have a terrific headache.*
Weeks short of witnessing Victory
in Europe, the president dies.
A massive stroke.

April 28, 1945

Here and there, dandelions pierce
sooty soil between the fallen stones
of Europe's towns. April brings hope
in leaky wicker baskets. Death
evident in varied forms.

On Italy's side of Lake Como the odor
of baby grass mingles with that of burnt rubber.
Partisans stop a German convoy. Hiding
in a truck—Mussolini, wearing a Nazi uniform.
They arrest him.

Clara Petacci joins Il Duce. Partisans execute
dictator and mistress, drive to Milan, dump
the corpses on the piazza, hang them by the feet
from the girders of an Esso station—For
modesty, Clara's skirt is tied at the knees.

Days before capture—
a foreboding. Mussolini wrote
to Rachele, his wife, urging her
to flee Italy, signing the letter
your Benito.

April 30, 1945

When news of Mussolini's execution reaches
Hitler, his mind sets on suicide, dreading
capture more than death.
He burrows in his Führerbunker
fifty feet below the Reich Chancellery,

right in the middle of Berlin—Allies never suspect.
Concrete walls sixteen-feet thick surround
the subterranean cave. With the Red Army
choking Berlin in steel tentacles, the Führer
sees no future. Marriage no longer hinders

the Nazi warlord's grand design.
In the windowless room still smelling
of wet cement, with Goebbels as witness,

Adolph Hitler and Eva Braun swear they are
of pure, un-contaminated Aryan blood.

A somber meal follows. Hitler is merry, others not.
To test the potency of potassium cyanide, Hitler tries it
on his beloved German shepherd. Death—near instantaneous.
He orders Blondi's pups shots. The dead dogs are dragged
four flights up and buried under Russian artillery fire.

Third Reich women accept their fates. Eva
embraces pistol and poison. Frau Goebbels asks
the SS dentist to inject her children with morphine.
When time comes she will crush ampoules
of cyanide into the six young mouths as they sleep.

Adolph rethinks suicide.
Unaware, bunker inmates light cigarettes
drink, crank the phonograph. SS guards
sneak naked girls in their quarters.
Enraged, Hitler stops the celebration.

Macabre silence. A shot.
Faint smell of gunpowder.
Bride and groom dead.
He, with a hole in his head.
She, with glass in her mouth.

Guards pour jerry cans of precious petrol
over the newlyweds. Cremation stretches
over two hours. Hot ashes, teeth, bits of bones
are scooped and interred in the windy, crater-
pitted area near Blondi and her pups.

April 16, 1945

When Emmanuel dies my mother
is in a hospital. Louis and I
are with friends so as not to burden our
grandmother who cares
for our little brother.

No one tells us.
We return. Our baby—dead for days—buried

in the ancestral plot beside the village church.
Papa in China never met his youngest son
born after he left.

In February, Emmanuel blew three candles
stuck in a one-egg-no-butter wartime cake.
A tablecloth draped over his empty crib barely shrouds
his homemade toys hidden beneath. The wooden boat
with the burlap sail, the wine cork pontoon, the rag dog.

Below our bedroom window—where Emmanuel
buried bulbs in his pocket garden—yellow flowers
peek. Beyond the daffodils spreads the orchard—
pink and white froth on pallbearer legs.
Beyond that, by the river, willows weep.

The Americans are coming.
We drag a table to the courtyard, bring out
glasses, a bottle of wine, practice a smile.
How does a three-year-old
prepare for death?

TURKEY

Longshoremen on strike.
For a week we watch our wooden crates
on a dock, covered by cargo nets.

First to board the Turkish ship is a herd of sheep.
My brother and I count the French farm animals.
Where will they find grass on the Mediterranean Sea?

On day three, when we hear the sad cries below
deck, we know these animals will end
up as mutton on the dining room plates.

The ship glides into the Bosphorus at dusk.
Istanbul glows as if drizzled with gold powder.
The warm air holds the smell of roasted sesame.

Also, the prayers of muezzins singing from fragile
minarets against a painted sky. On land, Papa awaits
us. A reunion after a four-year separation.

The Chinese embassy in Ankara—a gray building in a gray
city. On Sundays the military parades. Pedestrians, office
workers, street sweepers salute, stand at attention.

Even on hot days, soldiers wear coats frayed at the bottom.
I notice because I'm eight and my eyes are close to the ground.
On our way to school, children make skinny eyes, sing chin-chin-chow.

They throw stones at us. The parents throw stones at us.
Papa gives us camel-hair paint brushes. He rubs a black stick
in water to make ink. We try to please, hold the brush straight.

The tip makes a tiny point before spreading into a squirrel tail.
Our hands grow stiff. Our calligraphy is poor. Papa is strict.
At home we speak French, at the embassy we try Chinese.

We learn a few words of Turkish.
We're not confused
but it's hard.

VIVE LES AMÉRICAINS

MY NEAR EPIC VOYAGE TO AMERICA

My mother was nine months pregnant when we set out for America, in December 1946. Mama had fake papers stating she wasn't due for another three months. No ship captain wanted to deliver a baby in the middle of the Atlantic, in winter. "After all," she told us, "I was six months pregnant when I applied for the passport. Not my fault it took so long." This was *un petit mensonge,* not a mortal sin.

Papa had a job at the United Nations, and was awaiting us in New York. Before leaving, Mama showed us a brochure about the Île de France, a luxury liner, with a ballroom tall as a cathedral. Crystal chandeliers hung from the ceiling, even a merry-go-round on the deck. How was such a thing possible? I toned down my excitement. I had announced I didn't want to go.

The trip would not be a total loss as I planned to write a book about it. On the first page of the green leather diary Mama had given me, I printed: My Epic Voyage to the New World. I wanted a Jules Verne title.

On the second page, in cursive, I entered a passenger list. Nicolette, French, job: mother, age unknown. Nani, Armenian, job: grandmother, also concert pianist, very old. Louis, half Chinese, no job, seven. Claire, half Chinese, job: writer, nine. I referred to myself by name in case of shipwreck. I didn't want to be anonymous. We all had brown eyes and black hair except my mother who was blonde with blue eyes behind her glasses. She could have been adopted.

The official who stamped Mama's forged papers must have been blind, or his mother never told him where babies came from. Mama looked enormous. Her fake fur coat didn't even button. We all wore big clothes, and on the ride from Paris we couldn't even move to scratch our noses. We arrived at the port of Cherbourg at dark.

Sailors rushed us into a wobbly rowboat. I almost fainted when they put down their oars and stopped near a black mountain floating on black water. Everything seemed wrapped in dark material. Nani, who was not religious, made the sign of the cross. I poked Mama in the ribs, but she looked away. I refrained from commenting on the folly of this expedition; the ominousness of the situation was too obvious.

Upon climbing the swaying ladder, we found ourselves in a tar-smelling tunnel. A nice sailor, who spoke French with a Marseille accent, explained the ship had been mobilized to carry troops during WWII and had not yet been converted back for civilian use. The tarpaper served as a curfew curtain during trips from England to North Africa.

"What about the ballroom with the chandeliers?"

"Chandeliers?" The sailor laughed.

"What about the merry-go-round?"

"Merry-go-round?" More laughter.

The ship took a dip, and I vomited over my new shoes. A horrible thing to do as it brought attention to ourselves, and that's exactly what Mama had warned us against. She said if anyone found out about her advanced condition, we'd be thrown off the ship—a terrifying thought as some white stuff floated on the Atlantic. I didn't know if it was ice or something that would eat us.

We spent our first night on bunk beds in a dormitory, as the walls between cabins had been torn down to accommodate troops.

"I'm not going to like America, and I don't want to learn English," I announced that night. In his last letter Papa said he had found a house, and we would share it with another family. "Sharing a house with another family is a very, very bad idea," I added.

"Think of it as a wonderful adventure in a brand-new world," Nani said from her bunk below mine.

The captain found out Mama's secret on the second day. He panicked.

Being a good man, he didn't toss us into the freezing ocean. Instead, he gathered his hat and maps and moved out of his cabin to let the four of us move in. He even provided three cots. That night, Mama wouldn't let her mother sleep on a cot, so they fought for a while. Nani gave up out of exhaustion. She ended up in the captain's narrow wooden bed. Neither slept, my mother with her huge belly due to discomfort, and my grandmother because of guilt.

The whole thing was acceptable except for two problems: the smell that came from a W.C. with a sliding door and the level of the water rising and falling on the other side of the porthole. Both things caused me to throw up, and this triggered a chain reaction with the others. "My darling," Mama patted my head appeasingly. "I can't do a thing about the ship's movements. You don't have to look out. Just close your eyes."

I mentioned the bad odor. She squeezed through the narrow door and, while holding on to the washbasin, showed us the culprit. "It's an English soap," she said.

"No wonder it stinks," Louis and I said in unison.

"Don't say that. The English are very clean." Mama unwrapped the thing and showed us a pink object. "It's called *Leaf boo ye.*" She removed her glasses to translate the small print on the Lifebuoy wrapper. "Royal Disinfectant Soap. It kills microbes and prevents epidemics of typhoid, dysentery and yellow fever. Hmm. It contains carbolic acid."

"Carbolic acid, carbolic acid," Louis and I chanted.

The portholes had no latches, but the bathroom had a chain with a handle. I made my voice calm and polite. "Can we flush that pink soap down the toilet?"

"Absolutely not. Soap is a luxury."

To get away from the soap, each morning we went for "fresh air" in the asphalt tunnel. Weighed down by kilos of winter clothes, no wind could sweep us off the deck.

"We look like the Michelin man's kids," I said.

"Maybe a bit. Does that make me Madame Michelin?"

The ballroom consisted of long tables and benches to pretend it was a dining room. On the rare days we visited there, we spooned down bifty (beef tea) and square crackers with pinholes called Sal teens (Saltines). No one talked much as we were all a bucket away from nausea. The captain delighted in seeing my mother still pregnant under her heavy coat. He greeted her with, "Tout va bien, Madame?" and Mama answered, "Très bien, merci."

To pass the time, we played cards, and Nani made us do finger exercises so our piano hands wouldn't get flabby. At night, she told us stories she knew by heart—Ali Baba and Sinbad, also stories about ruthless Cossacks on the rampage. Mama tried to stop her from telling us these bloody tales. Once, when I complained more than usual, my grandmother told us the story of the brave children of Sparta.

"So the boy kept his pet fox under his shirt, never complaining. At the end of the school day the fox had chewed up his entire stomach and had started on the entrails."

"Please don't talk about those idiot Spartans," Mama burst out.

"Nicolette, I'm teaching them a lesson, and it's a good distraction no?"

Nani grew up in Armenia but had been forced to attend Russian schools. Her stories didn't end well, unlike Mama's tales that always ended happily and didn't give anybody nightmares. My mother also read to us Courteline and other French humorists. One story involved a timid man who enhanced his reputation by boasting he had double muscles. For some reason, this made her laugh until tears fogged her glasses. After she had regained control of herself, I thought it a good time to again bring up my big worry.

"What if we hate the people we're going to share a house with?"

"Fear not," Mama kissed my hair. "We'll be one big, double-muscle family."

We all laughed. I forgot to not laugh.

The Atlantic acted with vindictive fury for nine days, sending giant waves against the tar paper, turning it into icy black walls. Minutes before gliding into New York Harbor, the ocean behaved; we touched foot in New York Harbor on a clear, freezing December day.

While waiting to debark, I made a second entry in my book. *Arrival in the New World. Spotted Papa on the dock. He's wearing a gray hat and looks elegant.*

Papa gave us big hugs and packed us in his new Ford. He could barely close the trunk of the car over our jammed luggage. From the back seat I could smell the stinking soap in Mama's suitcase.

AMERICA

Icy winter winds slap our faces as we
approach our new house. Papa helps
unpack our bags. He shows us little
rooms with no beds, reserved for clothes.

At night, a slit in the curtains —
trees form upended crystal chandeliers.
Air fingers play the harp on branch tips
trapped in icy flacons.

From above, an aluminum
discus illuminates
dancing dandruff
from the sky.

By dawn, flakes
cram the window sill
and a baptismal drop cloth
covers the landscape.

While we slept snow drifted
against the door,
holding us captive
on our first day in America.

SHARING A HOUSE

The family we shared the house with, though French, spoke English fluently. My parents had known the couple in Paris during their days as students and Scout leaders. They had lost touch, but the formation of the United Nations reconnected them. The younger daughter had changed her name from Arabelle to Fleur, but her parents had kept their Scout names from *The Jungle Book*. Everyone called him Baloo and her Louva. We called them Oncle Baloo and Tante Louva, even though we were not related.

Days after our arrival, Marianne was born. By the time Mama and the new baby came home from the hospital, Louis and I knew our new address by heart. Five, six, four, Laurelton Boulevard, Long Beach, Long Island, New York. We practiced *Long Bitch, Long iss-land, Nous York.* Fleur helped us get it right. She didn't make fun of our English. Not wanting us to start school in the middle of the year, and the middle of an Arctic winter, my parents decided to let us stay home until September.

This meant a nine-month vacation.

Louis and I jumped with joy at this announcement. Having forgotten to not jump, I added, "That's too bad." Fleur didn't understand the meaning of no school. Being taught at home, she enjoyed year-round vacation. Tante Louva offered to instruct us along with her daughter. In my book I wrote, "I don't want to show too much enthusiasm, but I think school with Fleur will be fun."

Baloo worked nights as a translator, so we had to be quiet during the day while he slept. I learned not to yell and not to jump down the stairs three steps at a time. We tried to talk in subdued tones. This huge inconvenience didn't prevent us from having a good time. Weeks after our arrival, a truck delivered a wooden crate with our things. Louis showed Fleur his oilcloth Scotty dog and I let her hold my Snow White doll, gone bald from over-combing. Fleur didn't have dolls. Instead, she possessed laundry baskets bursting with plush animals. She also had a live cat. Animals that didn't have jobs were called pets, she informed us. Mimi Mouchti didn't even have to kill mice.

Because she had never gone to school, Fleur acted differently from anyone I knew. For one thing, she didn't know how to lie. I assigned myself the task of tutoring her in this basic survival skill. How would she manage when she stepped into the real world? I asked Louis to help but he wasn't good at lying himself. Once, when Fleur broke a Bavarian beer stein, I made her promise to deny it. She couldn't even perform that simple assignment. I worried about her.

Louva called her school La Zécole. La Zécole had no arithmetic. Too bad. However, it included some eccentric things we had never heard of, such as rhythm. On the first day, she played a tune on the piano and told us to be butterflies. Fleur grabbed a scarf and flew around the room, stopping by a chair or table pretending it was a flower. If you've never done this before, it's not easy. Louis and I stood stiffly by, but Fleur danced so freely, lifting her legs high and throwing her head back with such abandon that, bit by bit, we loosened and bounced around the living room as noiselessly as possible. Nani said she could hear us from the garden, and we sounded like wooly mammoth babies.

Oncle Baloo didn't have a car. When he came home at dawn, he walked the couple of miles from the train station and, before going to sleep, drew a picture of a bear and wrote the time he wanted to be awakened. He attached the drawing on the door of his bedroom with a transparent ribbon that had sticky stuff on one side. We stood on tiptoes to see the daily bears in their varied poses and funny facial expressions. If we woke him before the posted time, he came out like a hungry grizzly and Louis and I slid down the stairs and hid. Fleur stood her ground. She didn't know when to be scared.

For the drawing class, Fleur brought out a shoebox filled with delicious colored pencils. They shone like flowers and smelled of wood shavings. Even though she had favorites—red, black and turquoise— she didn't hide them from us and even allowed me to use them until the points shrunk. She then sharpened them with a gadget and let me use them again. I had never seen such generosity. During the war, Nani used her Swiss Army knife to cut pencils in half. Tante Louva gave us each a sheet of paper and told us to illustrate a story as she made it up. Fleur covered the whole page within minutes. Louis and I drew pictures in squares slightly larger than postage stamps.

"Fill the page," Tante Louva said. "Don't be afraid. Use the whole space."

In France, paper and rubber had been requisitioned by the Germans. We had no tires on our bikes. Without erasers, mistakes turned into disasters. Ink came in little bottles. Our pens had sharp removable tips. A leak was a catastrophe.

Fleur said not to worry about mistakes. "If you draw a dragonfly and it doesn't look like one, make it into a fairy."

"A fairy? I can do that?"

After a while, Louis and I learned to fill a whole sheet in one sitting. We also learned to make three-headed monsters out of blue, yellow and red modeling clay. This soft, sweet-smelling substance differed from the clay we scooped out from the river when the village cows finished drinking. Our clay was brownish. We formed small clumps into spheres and, to give them color, rolled them in chalk dust from the school blackboard rags. The sun dried our marbles. Fleur's marbles were miracles.

In America, you couldn't buy one egg. You had to buy a dozen. They came in special trays with twelve compartments. Fleur had several of these filled with transparent gems. Some marbles were opaque, others clear with colored spirals trapped inside them. When held to the light the colors changed. I didn't know a single person could own such a marvelous collection. She let us play with all of them.

Tante Louva wisely waited a week to introduce us to her movement lesson. She sat at the piano and played some very odd notes. Nani didn't cover her ears but quietly slipped out into the garden. Mama took baby and bassinet into the kitchen, closing two doors between us.

"You have to decide from the sounds you hear whether you are a rodent, an insect, a damsel in distress or a snake slithering down a tree." Tante Louva's hands galloped up and down the keyboard. I never figured out how her music didn't wake Baloo, yet my talking in a normal tone brought down the grizzly.

When we heard snake music, Louis climbed to the top of the stairs. A brave thing to do as the staircase was adjacent to the bear's den. Fleur and I followed and, guided by the music, the three of us dropped on our bellies and crawled down the stairs, head first. The fear of Baloo emerging from his room, his red hair sticking out at funny angles, caused me fits of repressed giggles that hurt my stomach more than the speedy descent down the twenty-two steps.

In spring, our double-muscle family moved to a bigger house in Glen Cove. A columned porch hugged three-quarters of the house, and two round towers guarded the roof. Oaks grew on the hillside, and birches leaned this way and that in the flower garden. Oncle Baloo slept better as we spent hours outdoors chasing each other with bows and suction-tipped arrows.

On Saturdays, we explored the garden, and Oncle Baloo taught us about plants and animals. Now, instead of tying threads to June bugs, I carried a drawing pad and sketched them. Instead of cutting worms to see the pieces squirm, I learned about invertebrates. Fleur told us the names of birds in French and English. On Sundays, Fleur grabbed a section of the newspaper and spread it out on the part of the floor that had a carpet. We got on our stomachs and she translated Prince Valiant to us as we looked at the pictures.

Papa was busy commuting to Lake Success every day. Chinese lessons grew far apart. We had outgrown the thin paper books about Little Dog and Little Cat, and our efforts at calligraphy were a great disappointment to Papa. He turned his gaze to the Olympics. He told us with practice we could become disciplined, supple athletes. Besides teaching us the Australian crawl, he built us swings, parallel bars, trapeze rings, and stilts for balance. He also bought us bicycles and roller skates.

Nani resumed our piano lessons. I learned to play a Chopin Berceuse. Louis practiced Debussy's Golliwog's Cakewalk. When Marianne slept, Mama read us French translations of Shakespeare, Mark Twain, and James Fenimore Cooper. The adults respected each other's domains, indoors for the women, outdoors for the men.

The flower garden caused some conflict. Baloo believed in a wild environment with untamed forsythia bushes and irises growing where they chose. Papa preferred flowerbeds and trimmed shrubbery. Once, while Baloo slept, my father, using his new tools, cut and pruned several trees and all the bushes.

"Fuyun, my dear friend, what possessed you?" Baloo exclaimed when he woke.

"I only did what needed to be done," Papa answered calmly.

"Nature thrives when left to its own course," Baloo said.

"Nature tends to grow wild and needs to be controlled."

The discussion revolved around the definition of the word *thrive*, reflecting both men's philosophies about gardening as well as their theories about education. The argument grew but remained civilized and ended in peace. After all, our fathers had been Scouts together, and both worked for the United Nations.

Although the size of the house allowed all of us to roam without getting into each other's way, there were rules. We shared the kitchen but had separate dining rooms. "This is the secret to our two families' peaceful cohabitation," Mama wrote her sister in France.

Although we all had access to the kitchen. Mama advised us to stay out of that room to avoid being in the way. I made some efforts but resented that Fleur was allowed to fix her own food in the morning.

One day, I watched her open a cabinet filled with small boxes. After selecting one, she took a sharp knife and cut the cardboard so it would open like shutters. Shiny paper lined the inside of the carton, which contained airy pellets. She opened the kitchen door and brought in the wire basket with four bottles of milk delivered that morning. She poured the milk straight from the bottle into the cardboard container, nearly spilling the cream that floated on top. I was aghast.

"The wax paper is waterproof," she said. I didn't believe her, but nothing leaked.

"Is this your little lunch?" I said in English, proud to have translated *petit déjeuner* in my head.

"You mean breakfast. Listen," she said. She raised the box to my ear. "Rice Krispies."

I heard little explosions.

"Try it." She handed me the container with a spoon and fixed herself another one.

Fleur also showed me how to put a slice of spongy bread into a silver machine and push down a lever. After a short while, a "toast" popped out.

We ate half a week's supply in the neutral territory of the kitchen.

Fleur prepared us for the holidays. In February, she showed us how to fold red paper in half and cut it in a way that, when opened, it was shaped like a heart. That month was icy cold. Snow kept us indoors for days in a row. One morning my mother bundled Marianne in a ton of blankets into her baby carriage and took Louis and me to buy boots. Fleur had the right footwear but came with us anyway. While Mama was helping my brother, a salesman brought me a pair to try on and asked if they felt good.

"No," I said, "they hurt my foot fingers."

"Toes." Fleur explained the proper translation for *doigts de pieds*.

I learned that in America, Easter bunnies hid the eggs. That made more sense than church bells dropping off hard-boiled eggs in the bushes. Either way, we got to color eggs, but the color came from the A&P, and we didn't have to boil onion skins to make red. I was delighted that the Americans chose the Fourth of July, my birthday, to celebrate the birth of their nation.

I liked the fact that the sky burst with fireworks on the day I was born. In Switzerland, my birthplace, that day was just an ordinary day.

When Fleur's older sister came home from college, she invited some of her friends to put on a play. They were archeology students interested in drama. Together, they transformed the barn into a theater. At dusk, Clairève lined the driveway with lanterns, and the audience, consisting of our two families, friends and neighbors, sat on chairs between two rows of flickering flames. Wearing sheets tied at the shoulders, Clairève and her friends introduced us to Greek drama under a yellow moon. The actors had painted white templar columns on either side of the tall barn door. At the end of the performance, a goddess appeared above the clouds. She spoke Greek behind a mask, and her waist-long hair glowed like exposed copper wire. After the show I sneaked into the barn and realized Fleur's sister had stood at the top of an extension ladder and had delivered her speech from the hayloft. Paper clouds hung from the rafters. I had been completely fooled.

No, the actors had created magic.

Under the barn, on the cliff side of the property, someone had dug a scary cave. Neither Fleur, Louis, nor I had dared explore it. One day, Clairève, wearing coveralls, marched into that dark hole with a full bucket and a large brush. Sitting on our heels, with the sun to our backs, we watched from afar as Clairève splashed plaster water against the black wall. "You are the shadows outside Plato's cave," she told us. After the wall dried, she marked it with a piece of coal. "Now I need to work by myself." She faced us, paintbrush in the air.

Days later, she dragged some logs for seats and invited us in. My eyes popped. Mount Olympus stood before us. Upon it, Clairève had painted Athena, Zeus, and minor gods reclining under an olive tree. The quiet, the coolness, the figures, the colors made us speechless. She had transformed a dangerous black hole into a place for the gods.

Before returning to school, Clairève and Baloo assembled several railroad ties to make us a fort. It was built like a log cabin without a roof.

In August, Nani and Mama, pushing Marianne in her carriage, walked Louis and me to St. Patrick's Elementary School and enrolled us for the fall semester. Fleur had become a sister to me, and I wanted her to start school with us. I worried she might be lonely by herself, but her parents thought otherwise. On Labor Day, I began a new section in my book. It read: "After a nine-month vacation, I almost look forward to long division and starting school in America."

CHICKEN WITH WORMS

I spoke some English before I knew it. My first English word was pull-over (*poule aux vers*). I didn't know it was English. I thought when my mother knitted us sweaters, she was knitting chicken with worms. My second English word was eider down. At night we kept warm under an édredon. It was made of a blanket-sized bag filled with chicken feathers. Apparently, the English made the same thing but filled their duvet with the soft down of Icelandic eider ducks.

After telling my mother (diplomatically) that it was embarrassing to walk to school with an escort that included a mother, a grandmother, and a baby, we were allowed to go by ourselves. School was walking distance from the old Victorian house our families rented. I was ten when I entered fifth grade. On the first day of class, Sister Theresa asked if anyone wanted to sit in the back of the room and help me with English. One hand went up. For the rest of the school year, Rosemary became my teacher. She had blonde hair. Glasses veiled her iris-blue eyes. I never saw her without her glasses, even at recess.

She showed no interest in dresses or party shoes (we wore uniforms and brown Oxfords) but dreamed of owning a pair of cowboy boots. She loved animals and wanted to be a veterinarian. Her other interests included American Indians and baseball. During recess she drew diamond shapes in the dirt and explained her favorite game to me. I tried to understand but never got the hang of it. She brought baseball cards to school and told me about Yogi Berra and Mickey Mantle. She could talk all day about the Yankees. Chief Joseph and Abraham Lincoln came close to her sports heroes in the list of people she admired. She read me stories about them. When the teacher assigned the above topics, I did well.

She was not awed by authority and often muttered under her breath words I wouldn't understand until the next grade. She told me the English language often made no sense. "For example," she said, "you pronounce rough and tough the same," she wrote *ruff* and *tuff*. "But," she added, "you can't say bread *duff*. It's bread dough, pronounced *doe*." English was also weird when it came to accents. "For example," she said, "you'd think if you said con**ver**tible, you'd also say com**for**table. You'd think, wouldn't you? You can't, you say **com**fortable." She marked the accented syllables with red pencil.

Rosemary got A-pluses on all her tests. She rarely read original texts but was well-versed in Classic Comics. "That's where the nuns get the material for our exams," she informed me. I didn't believe her. I couldn't imagine nuns reading comics.

Rosemary also instructed me in the use of idioms. She said I needed to know them so I could sound American. "These expressions don't always make sense," she warned me. "'Taking candy from a baby' means it's easy to do; 'eating like a bird' means having a small appetite. Well, babies bite your fingers off, and baby birds eat nonstop." She pushed her glasses up her nose and added, "Idioms are not important. You don't *have* to use them. If you use them right, you sound American; if you use them wrong, you sound like a dumb-dumb."

I wanted to sound American, so I practiced idioms as often as I could, and she helped me keep things straight: "Beating around the bush means to talk crooked," she instructed. "You said, 'hitting the bush around.' That means damaging shrubbery."

My English skills improved daily, and by the end of the first term, I could fight my own battles on the playground. I didn't have a rich vocabulary of insults, however, and found that when I called a classmate "cow" or "camel," they were amused rather than offended. On the other hand, telling someone they were a son of a female dog was very insulting. I didn't understand this as to me a puppy was a cute animal.

Once, during a horrible Latin class, Sister Josephina was explaining gender nouns. Rosemary was annoyed that everything had to be either feminine or masculine. I said that was the only thing I liked about Latin. In broken English, I explained that English was a camouflage language, and I was bothered by that.

"What do you mean?" she whispered.

"If I tell you I'm going to see my cousin, in French, I say *cousin* or *cousine*, and you know right away if it's a boy or a girl."

"That's a good thing about English," Rosemary said.

"No, it's not. You always have to ask a second question to find out, and you sound nosy." Nosy was a new word for me, I was practicing with it.

"Well, I like camouflage." She thought for a minute. "Does *everything* have a masculine and a feminine?"

"Of course, cup is feminine, *une* tasse, glass is masculine, *un verre*."

"What about potato?"

"Pomme de terre is a girl."

"Bean?"

"Haricot is a boy."

We burst out laughing, and Sister Josephina switched from Latin to English to send us to the principal. On the way there, Rosemary asked, "*Une* principal or *un* principal?" For some reason, this struck us as funny, and we got cramps from repressing mirth during Mother Superior's lecture.

At home, language was not a problem as we easily reverted to French. Outside was another matter. The vowels "e" and "i" bedeviled me as they sounded so different in so many words. I remember my first public embarrassment: we were at a Howard Johnson's restaurant, a rare event. After salivating over pictures of food, I ordered "apple pee à la mode." The waitress repressed a laugh. I knew I had said a stupid thing.

We had never heard of Halloween. Fleur and her family would be away for that day, but they told us to buy pails of candy and give out handfuls to people who came to the door that evening. If we didn't, they might throw eggs at the door "or worse." We sat in the living room, waiting for the doorbell to ring. When it did, I rushed to open the door. A well-dressed couple stood on the threshold. They didn't look like vandals. To be friendly, I invited them in, offering them comfortable chairs, cookies and drinks. My parents sat across the coffee table from them and conversed in English. "Should we serve them dinner?" Mama asked my father in French.

"Wait a bit," Papa answered.

He offered them cigarettes. The adults took turns looking at their watches. Louis and I sat on the floor, waiting for the ash at the end of the man's cigarette to fall on the rug. After a half-hour the adults had run out of things to talk about.

"Mr. Smith," the man told our father, "I didn't expect you to be Chinese."

"My name is Fuyun Hsu," Papa answered.

"We're so sorry." The man stood. "We were invited by a friend. He said we were to meet at Mr. Smith's house. We must have the wrong address."

Louis and I gave them bags of candy anyway.

WORDS

In America, to my immense relief, the Chinese lessons stopped completely. Our English improved daily, but we had to be extra careful of words that looked like French ones but had a different meaning. At the post office, I told the clerk, my mother demanded airmail stamps. Fleur explained that although *demande* meant "ask" in French, in English, demand was not polite. My mother had studied English in school. Baloo said she spoke fluently with a very good French accent. The funny thing is, he himself had an accent. Mama's background was academic, not culinary. At the corner of our street stood a mansion with a huge expanse of grass upon which life-sized plastic sheep grazed in all weather. We called it *la maison aux moutons.* I heard my mother give directions that included turning at the house with the muttons on the grass. Fleur said it should be "sheep on the lawn." She explained that animals were called one name when alive, and another when they became food. A baby cow was a calf, but on a plate, it became veal. "Never say a herd of beef," she warned me. Baloo, a linguist, overhead our conversation and explained that when William the Conqueror crossed the channel, he let the Saxon peasants raise cows, sheep and pigs, but the Norman cooks, in an attempt to raise English cuisine to a higher level, Frenchified their menus. They referred to meat as boeuf, mouton and porc; which became beef, mutton and pork.

FLYING LESSON

April winds, whispers of lilac
scent my hair.
Purple at my feet, velvet crocuses.

Apple petals like snow on grass.
Papa puts finishing touches on our tissue
paper kites. Mine's a dragonfly.

My brother's, a bumblebee. We run up
the slope, balls of strings in sweaty hands.
Don't drag them, Papa calls to us.

We wait for his signal, race downhill.
Our kites pull and yank. Sink and lift.
We gallop and tug. A mighty gust sweeps

dragonfly to sky, to sun
on a filament of light.
Remembering poor Icarus

I tighten the string, call it back.
But Papa, wiser than old Daedalus,
used home-stirred glue made of wheat flour,

not wax from the hive to secure the wings.
We're safe. I, and my dragonship, levitate—
treetops to puffy cloud streets.

Down below, Papa waves.
Fly, fly, he shouts.
Windborne, over ocean I soar

free as a migrating bird.
And I'll touch foot in Paris
in time for tea and a warm brioche.

POINT OF VIEW

Pont Mirabeau

At school in Paris, the children were mean, the teachers strict.
I hated la grammaire, l'orthographe, les conjugaisons.
From our third-floor apartment, between the trees,
I could see the Seine River flow, always sparkling.

Crossing the Pont Mirabeau, Mama let me and my brother stop,
stand on tip toes and wave to the barges approaching the bridge.
Families lived on these flat boats. Children my age ran between
mounds of sand or coal, and climbed on crates and burlap bags.

Some played hide and seek between the sheets that hung
from poles on the decks. Sometimes a dog on a leash barked
or a baby in a playpen cried. How I envied the children who
spent their lives on the river and never had to go to school.

The barges glided silently toward us and disappeared
under our feet, leaving behind long, white swallow-tails.
I so wished I were a boat-kid standing on a pile of bricks
and waving to the school children on the Mirabeau bridge.

Benchmark

Sitting on a city bench in Washington Square Park, I bite
into my sloppy egg salad sandwich. On my lap, the wooden
box with my histology slides—perfectly stained, ready to
hand in for midterm exams. Beside me three heavy books:

comparative anatomy, physics, inorganic chemistry. As my
lunch debris falls to ground, a feathered flock circles me.
How I envy the purple pigeons, and the old men at the chess
tables, oblivious of homework, laboratories and final exams.

WASHINGTON SQUARE TO 42ND STREET

To Allan

Hand-in-hand we walk from Washington
Square to 42nd Street. A wintry afternoon.
We're young. You offer to carry
my books. I refuse. You've got your own.
Your jacket's crammed under your arm
to show what a stoic you are.

A detour at 14th Street. You show me
Union Square, where, at sixteen, you made
socialist speeches and handed out pamphlets.
It takes us out of our way.
At the corner of 5th and 23rd, four gloved
and ear-muffed musicians draped in bright

garments beat their drums. The African garbs
remind you of Dian Fossey, who had her healthy
appendix removed before traveling to Tanzania.
It's a stupid thing to do, I tell you.
You disagree. *It's preventive medicine.*
Icy gusts blow from the river.

Smell of snow in the air. *Put on your jacket,*
I mention, **prevent** *pneumonia.* You're not
cold you claim—maybe so. Your hand is warm.
As we cross 29th Street, we pass a church.
I envy your belief in God, you say. I suspect
as a mathematician you seek absolute proof.

*Faith is not a rational thing. Look at those
dead trees*, I point with my chin, *soon
they'll be alive with infant leaves.
Doesn't that make you believe in God?
No*, you answer, *but I'm a reluctant atheist.*
34th Street darkens with the mass of the Empire.

A freezing breeze dislodges my scarf. I don't fix it,
not wanting to release my fingers from the cozy envelope
of your hand. I endure the cold St. Christopher medal
on my neck. We reach 42nd Street. You have enough for
a pizza slice from a corner stand. We bisect it with a
plastic knife. Cheese stretches between pieces.

Steam warms our faces. What sun there was
slipped away unnoticed. Time to part. You'll
tunnel west to New Jersey. I'll go the other way
under the East River to Queens.
Slowly, you let go my hand. I insert it
in my pocket to save the warmth.

HOW WE MET

You remember English class.
I remember biology.

You hated cutting up animals.
I borrowed your scalpel.

You were on the GI Bill, hungry to learn.
I was straight out of high school, hated homework.

Professor Pfeiffer read my essay
anonymously. You asked him for my name.

You fell in love with what I wrote.
I was just showing off.

Had never been in a bar,
should not have written about one.

You took me to Rocky's. We sat on barrels, feet
in sawdust. Chianti bottles dripping red candle wax.

It was actually what I had described. Now,
I think it wasn't an accident you chose that dive.

We had no money, no car, no free time. Yet,
we walked, rode subways, caught buses, saw plays.

We journeyed together,
we had a destination.

BEFORE WE MET

Your mom arrived on a boat
from Italy when she was three.

Her mother, small, loving and fierce,
raised eight strong, American children.

Her five sons, your uncles, all served in WWII.
In the army, the navy, and the air force too.

At twelve, you brought home a gun.
Grandma broke it with her bony hands.

Your mom married the "life of the party," a hard
worker, who knew nothing about tenderness.

When you were two, you refused
to say goodbye to your father's brother.

Dad wrapped a towel around
your neck—repeated the order.

You locked your lips. Uncle Al
saved you from strangulation.

After he left, you crossed your arms and in your
toddler voice boasted, *I didn't say goodbye.*

You broke your mother's heart when
without a word, you joined the Navy.

Years ago, someone asked me if your family
objected to me. I was curious. *Why?*

Because you're half Chinese.
It had never occurred to me they might.

YANKEE COLORS

Acrid smell of chrysanthemums
the crunch of feet on dried leaves—
walking on potato chips. We huddle
under a mohair blanket. Thermos coffee
steams our glasses as we watch
Notre Dame beat the hell out of Navy.

Translucent amber syrup poured over silver-dollar
pancakes in a roadside inn on our way to Middlebury
College. No one prepared me for autumn in Vermont.
No one told me about flaming trees,
about phantom colors that burn inside
my eyelids when I close my eyes.

Such reds are meant for flags to lead men
to battle. Such oranges—a solar eclipse—
should be viewed through smoked glass.
Such pinks, bordering on yellows
stolen from the finest silk kimonos
No one prepared me for these Yankee colors.

WINTER POOL

Your cousin from California visited in February,
when New York snow had turned yellow
from passing dogs. She said in Los Angeles
they had a pool and swam twelve months of the year.

That stuck with you as you pedaled
to teach your class. Your briefcase full
of math bounced on the uneven road
as you thought of turquoise waters.

Your mind made up, you came
home, shook snowflakes off your hair
and said: *Let's move to California. I'll get
a job, I'll learn to drive, we'll buy a car.*

You got a job,
you learned to drive,
we bought a van.
You were thirty-four.

GREEN VAN

Such a novelty in Hempstead, NY.
Crowds on the sidewalks peeking.
You standing proudly. Me scared to death.
You just got your license, barely able
to leave the dealer lot in February on icy roads.

And now you want to drive across
the continent with a four-year-old,
a toddler in diapers, and barbells
in the back of the van. Beds made from
poles and a stretch of canvas.

Camping across country.
Midnight arrivals.
Locating bathrooms by flashlight
searching for a green van when
everyone had a green van.

Ash in the coffee, lifting weights
to reach the cooler. You befriending
a fluffy bear cub, unaware of worried
mama at your back. Still, we had talks
by the fire, stars in the sky, laughter.

In mid-continent America—
total amnesia of the state,
the city or the restaurant.
It was Sunday, I remember that.
Dinner time.

Men in jackets and ties. Wives with white gloves,
groomed children. Cloth table covers. We enter
garbed in sweats and sneakers. Beth lines up the silver-
ware—under the table. Meal over, Christina climbs
on her velour chair, gargles, spits on the carpet.

We head for the door.

TOASTING MAMA ON VALENTINE'S DAY

On this day, we raise our
glasses to Mama who died
twenty-six years ago.
I didn't get to tell her…

Thank you, Mama, for your love of books,
for filling the long winter nights
with brave knights, troublesome Greek
gods, Shakespeare and Mark Twain—
in French—and all the poems you loved.

Thank you for wearing in public
the garish scarves and harlequin
skirts I made for you after you
taught me to knit and pedal your
new Singer machine.

Thank you for your sense of humor, and thank
you for calling us for a snack when Chinese
lessons with Papa ended up in tears. Also,
for suggesting to him that maybe we really
did not need to win Olympic medals.

Thank you for your free spirit. For teaching me
that eating a hot dog on Friday was less of a sin
than teasing my brother any day of the week. Thank
you for eating cookies I made when I mistakenly
used soap powder in lieu of sugar.

Thank you for showing me that a cup of cocoa
and buttered bread were good remedies
for small miseries. Thank you for letting
me know that being kind was important,
but I didn't need to be kind to everybody.

Tyrants and fanatics were the work of the devil
you said, and at times, it was important to speak up.
You favored the underdog. In your eighties, when
heckled for defending gay rights, you smiled, waved
your banner and wore the insults like a gold medal.

Merci d'avoir été ma mère.

NINE ELEVEN

At dawn, a red–tailed
window. The house
did not die. It fell to

On my way to the hospital
A Boeing 767 cannonballs
in Manhattan. Three-thousand

Paradise Valley Hospital, CA.
My father's room dark.
He who collected elegant

His once tanned arms
So thin. The hands that
to ride bikes, now lie

On the wall-installed TV
the other tower. Fatally wounded
Nebula particles fall and rise

Cameras record the death
Plastic tubes enter and
Monitors beep his vital

My father, the news junkie
Nurses ask me to switch off the
the roommate complains.

Donor blood siphoned
Papa's veins. The hemo
its pink plasma walls

In the City's clogged arteries
to paths of least obstructions.
gridlocked on a bed, barely

Diagonally, across the country
Shrouded by veils of toxic dust
Unlike the hawk that fell

No one rises.

PACIFIC TIME

hawk dove against my
didn't crumble, the bird
ground and flew to sky.

the 6 a.m. news.
into one of the Tall Towers
miles across the continent.

Filipina nurses pray in chapel.
The food untouched.
shoes, wears purple booties.

white as rice noodles and thin.
guided us when we learned
shipwrecked by his side.

a second plane penetrates
the twin brothers collapse.
choke the tough island city.

of the World Trade Center.
exit Papa's flattened body.
signs in horizontal zigzags.

turns to the wall.
news. I lower the volume. Still
I draw the curtain, as if it mattered.

through clear plastic fills
pouch nears empty,
cling to each other.

people like corpuscles gush
My world-traveler father, now
a mound, wearing a paper gown.

steel liquefies, stones pulverize.
men, women dive to hot pavement.
to ground, at dawn on Nine-Eleven

No one flies.

INHERITANCE

At twenty, my father leaves China to study
in Paris. His scholarship allows no luxury.
He acquires French while studying law, grows
mushrooms in a basement, teaches himself to make
meager but tasty meals. He dresses well, travels,
makes friends easily—always pushes his limits.

As a little girl, Mama watches drops of water slide
on the window pane. She hopes for a deluge. If so,
she doesn't have to tag along with Grandpapa on a dreary
walk with umbrella. She can stay home, pull the curtain,
sink into an old cracked-leather chair with a book
that weighs bricks. When sad parts fog her glasses

she removes them briefly, replaces them quickly.
She has her father's blue eyes, his myopia.
At night she copies poems from authors she loves.
Fills school notebooks with careful cursive
lines. Her pen dipped in a glass inkwell
occasionally adds unexpected punctuation.

After she marries my father, she follows
him on four continents, traveling with
five children. He always goes ahead
to find a place for his growing family.
All along Mama drags her notebooks.
Notebooks we know nothing about.

The love of adventure might have made
Papa a rebel, but he obeyed laws, stopped
for red lights at the dead of night with no
traffic in sight. It was my mother who jay-
walked, took part in demonstrations, and let us
skip school now and then, for no good reason.

My father loved firecrackers, and Westerns.
My mother did not. Her passion was reading.
I seek adventure and follow rules
like Papa, with some exceptions.
From Mama I inherited a love
of poetry and an addiction to words.

THE PERFECT DEATH OF A TAI CHI MASTER

2005: Two days after Christmas, my father, with the sun on his face, drifts off to sleep in his recliner. Outside, purple finger-tips emerge from the early bloom of the magnolias he planted. My three sisters and I are eating croissants when the breathing stops. Snow Blossom, my six-year-old niece, is first to notice. *Is Papa dead?* she asks.

1905: Fuyun Hsu is born in Wuxi, China. Fuyun means Double Cloud.

2000: The doctor asks Papa what is the secret of his good health. *Two things,* he answers, *A glass of wine with every meal and, now and then, a good cigar.*

1987: *Dr. Hsu, what is the secret of your long marriage?* his tai chi students ask. *Two words,* he tells them, *Yes, dear.* He doesn't mention it's my mother who uses the magic words.

1995: One February morning, Papa calls me and says Mama won't get up. The doctor arranges for hospice home care. My parents don't understand the implication. To make her smile, Fuyun promises to be baptized. She dies at home. He keeps his promise, at age ninety. He's christened by a Filipino priest who could be his grandson.

1996: Papa removes a family photo from a frame and replaces it with one of Bill Clinton. When the candidate comes to National City, my sister Marianne takes Papa to see him. They stand hours in the sun. She buys him a green hat. Papa shakes Clinton's hand and says, *I got my citizenship so I could vote for you.* The candidate moves ahead through the crowd then comes back to shake my father's hand a second time. Marianne snaps a picture. Papa wants prints. The photo clerk calls and asks if we really want multiple copies of a baseball cap. Of course, Papa answers.

1925: At age twenty, Fuyun receives a scholarship to the Sorbonne. He travels from China to Paris—studies law. He arrives early for class, sits in the front row to follow the lecture in French. When he spots a young woman standing at the back of the amphitheater, Fuyun offers her his seat. Her name is Nicolette Babaian Laloy.

1937: Because he's not Catholic, Fuyun and Nicolette are married in a side altar of Notre Dame. On July 4th, I am born in Geneva, Switzerland, where Papa works at the League of Nations.Three days after my birth, a gunshot incident triggered by Japan occurs on the Marco Polo Bridge near Beijing. China is at war with Japan.

1939: My brother Louis is born. On September 1st at dawn, Hitler's armies invade Poland. World War II begins. The triggering incident is code-named Canned Goods.

1941: The League of Nations collapses. Papa is offered a job in China. We move to Paris. While waiting for his passport, Papa makes puppets and stages elaborate shows for Louis, me, and our cousins. On June 22, he is on the Trans-Siberian Railway. The train stops near Moscow. Loudspeakers blare. Hitler launches Operation Barbarossa. His tanks crash into Russia. The Eurasian continent is split in half. Papa is on one side, we on the other. He's on his way to Chungking, we remain in France. I have to take good care of Mama, Papa told me. She's carrying a little brother or sister inside her. I am four years old.

1945: After my eighth birthday, we reunite with Papa in Ankara. He teaches my brother and me Chinese. The lessons end in tears. Mama says maybe we are too young. He wants us to dance like Cossacks. We fall on our butts. We disappoint him. Turkish children and their parents don't like us. Our neighbor, in his pajamas, jumps out of his window with a kitchen knife and punctures our ball when it falls into his yard. We're not supposed to show our emotions, but we cry in public.

Earlier that year, we cried in public and in private when our three-year-old baby brother died. Mama was in the hospital with a burst appendix. Louis and I were staying with friends. When we returned, our baby brother was already buried. We never said goodbye. Papa never saw his second son. We don't talk about Emmanuel.

1980: My parents retire in California. They buy a house. They also buy a narrow strip of earth in Glen Abbey. A surprise, because at home we never speak of death. We say autumn leaves, not dead leaves, and cul-de-sac (bag's ass in French) instead of dead end.

1947: Mama is almost thrown off the ship when the captain notices how pregnant she is. She lies and says she's not due for three months. In fact, she's nine months pregnant. Papa awaits us in New York. He has a car and commutes to Lake Success where he works for the United Nations. My sister, Marianne, is born days after our arrival, Vivian the next year, and Sylvie the year after that.

1954-1970: My father travels to areas of conflict: Cameroon, Togoland and the Congo. He is a negotiator and a peacemaker. My mother and my three sisters join him in Ethiopia. They have horses and Mama teaches French. She falls in love with her young students, among them the grandchildren of Emperor Haile Selassie. Later, in New York, she teaches the daughters of Malcolm X. This is the best time of her life. In Ivory Coast, Papa studies with a tai chi master from Taiwan, and becomes a master himself.

1950: We live in Greece. A young man rides his bike to see me. Papa forbids me to speak to him. *Why?* I ask the negotiator, the peace-maker. *Because I say so*, he answers. Mama tells me it has to do with the Chinese tradition of filial obedience. I say, *We're not in China, we're in Athens, the cradle of democracy.* Mama says her father was the same, and he was French. How's that for logic?

2002: Papa no longer does tai chi with his students but sits on a folding chair, as he watches them. *Repeat the third sequence,* he says politely. Papa has mellowed.

2003: Our daughter Christina practices tai chi under the purple magnolia. Papa, a Burberry scarf around his neck, watches from the living room. *Movement ninety-six should be inside the left foot,* he calls out.

2004: On our way to Denny's, Papa tells my husband, *I may be 99 on the outside but inside I feel 25.* Allan says he is 18 on the inside. I sit in the backseat; I could be their grandmother. Allan's hair turned white years ago. My father's remains black, no wrinkles, but he's shrunk. Papa's glad Peggy, his special waitress, has moved and doesn't see him in a rented wheelchair. He accepts being wheeled to the UCSD library for his Chinese book donation. He enjoys the honor. Our two daughters, UCSD graduates, are awed by parking on campus in spaces marked Reserved for Hsu Family.

1995: Fuyun takes over Nicolette's class after her death. The students get a kick—their French teacher is Chinese. Every June, he combines the tai chi and French classes for an end-of-year gala. He makes them sing in Chinese and writes plays for them. My three sisters are summoned from the East Coast to create drums, swords, even a magpie bridge across the Milky Way. Papa's great-grandson plays Mulan's four-year-old brother.

1998: To renew his driver's license, my father practices the questions. He sees with only one eye. We hope he fails the vision exam. He passes but wants a retake of the DMV photo—still vain at ninety-three.

2001: We take Papa to the ER. On September 11, from his hospital room, I watch the Twin Towers collapse like a child's block construction. The nurses ask me to switch off the TV. I can't. With my foot, I nudge the door shut. Papa, a news junkie all his life, turns his head to the wall. He comes home after blood transfusions.

2005: A young Filipino caregiver moves in with my father. Papa teaches him French songs. November 27th. My father is 100. We celebrate his birthday three times, with family, friends, and his students. Each time, he raises his glass and leads the singing toast he composed. In the Chinese tradition, he reminds us, he is actually 101.

Two days after Christmas, the tai chi master, with the sun on his face, drifts off while my sisters, Snow Blossom, and I eat croissants by his side.

BLACK MARKER

A month after Valentine's day.
At a White House briefing
on Corona Virus, the 45th
President reads from a prepared text.
A reporter notices he used
a Sharpie pen to blacken

"Corona," and wrote over it
in caps, "CHINESE Virus."

More than 3,000 hate incidents
target Asians between
March 16, 2020
and
March 16, 2021

Today on my walk, a cascade
of lavender lanterns dangle—
face down—over a redwood fence,
early gift from the Brazilian tree
and a neighbor I've never met.

Further on, orange puddles of soft
petals have opened after the rain.
Vert-de-gris filigree hug the blooms,
no distance between poppies
and leaves. No distance at all.

A woodpecker departs his tree
for a phone pole. One affixed
with a metal barrel to provide
echo and double the impact
of his coded S … O - - - S …

On this day in Atlanta, GA.
Eight people shot dead.
Seven women
six of them
Asian

.

WHERE IS MY AMERICA?

No longer in high places. Not on the mountaintop.

My America is
under a bridge where a man
with a Veteran cap
hangs a mirror on his shopping cart
and trims his beard with plastic scissors
for his new job as a bag boy.

My America is
the studio apartment of a young high
school teacher who shares it with a student
so he can graduate. The boy's jobless
mom having moved back to Georgia
with his younger siblings.

My America is
the hospital where a girl of ten awaits
a transplant. The donor: a stranger
whose kidney is being flown in an ice-
packed cooler marked Human Tissue
from a thousand miles away.

My America is
a school bus crammed with rebellious teens traveling
from Virginia to NYC to hear *Carmen*. Their teacher,
a middle-aged woman, changed the life of a black youth.
A trailer park boy—volcanic temper, police record, time
in solitary—now a baritone at the Metropolitan Opera.

My America is
the facility where
a caregiver used her
back to carry elderly
patients to the rooftop
when water rose.

My America is
the inn where pilgrims
are told, "There is room
for you. With or without
proper papers there will
be bread, water and a bed."

PAPA'S NOTES ON CITIZENSHIP IN AN EMAIL DATED MARCH 29, 1996

This was a great day when officially I became an American citizen!

As instructed by the INS I promptly arrived at the meeting place at 8:30 a.m., accompanied by Allan, Claire and Danny, Allan driving. The meeting place was:

Scottish Rite Center
1895 Camino del Rio South
San Diego, CA 92108

When we arrived at the Parking we saw a long, long line of men and women and children starting from the gate of the Center extending along the border of the immense parking lot to an almost invisible end! I estimated these waiting people to be a thousand, but Danny said maybe 2 thousand. I docilely added myself to the end of the queue, thinking that it would take hours to move, before my turn to reach the Center's entrance!

To my unexpected surprise, I was inside the Center in half an hour, in front of Desk no. 1 with all necessary papers, and was instructed to take a seat at the 8th row in this immense masonic hall. The immensity did not strike me any more. And waiting there, were hundreds of applicants who had arrived after me and had yet to check in!

The ceremony of Swearing-in was scheduled at 10 am. A broadcast voice announced we had 20 minutes yet before the ceremony, "please feel free to have a refreshment at the lobby". At 10, the ceremony was presided over by an official of the US District Court: A lady in a black robe made a lengthy speech about the grandeur of the great country and the spirit of the US flag. She welcomed the applicants from 48 countries, and congratulated them on becoming new citizens of the USA. After the ceremony of Oath Taking, and the National Anthem, we were asked to line up to receive our Certificate of Naturalization.

But here was the last and best episode of the Swearing-in day: So as instructed, I proceeded to table #1 to receive my Certificate of Naturalization. There were already a dozen persons lined up before me, when suddenly I heard a voice: "Dr. HSU"! It came from an immigration officer behind table #7. It was Virginia Reyes, one of my Taichi students! The time it took me to walk out of my line to shake hands with her, 3 more persons added themselves to my line, and I was once again at the end of the line. Fortunately, Virginia came to me, took me out from the waiting line, and gave me the Certificate carrying my name, while the 15 people in my line still waiting. It was good to have a student of mine working inside the INS!

PAPA'S RINGS

My father made up his mind to live to be one hundred. By the time he reached the century mark, his fingers had grown thin, and he wore his wedding band, along with my mother's, around his neck on a cord with a red-white-and-blue pen. His birthday was on Thanksgiving Day, but he held on to life through Christmas, when my brother and three sisters would come to visit from the East Coast.

After a first retirement near Grasse, on the French Riviera, my parents moved to San Diego, California, minutes from my home.

After Papa's funeral, we looked for his rings.

My siblings searched through drawers, boxes and closets. Even rolling aside the lead-weight, wool rug my parents had commissioned when they lived in Addis Ababa. The rings were nowhere to be found. My brother had to leave, but my sisters extended their stay until the Monday after Christmas.

I could have looked for the lost objects after their departure but my sisters wanted to save me the trouble. They spent the entire Sunday in my father's garage with the door down, transferring trash from one bag to another and rummaging through mountains of boxes. I joined them as an observer rather than a participant.

While going through a carton labeled miscellaneous, Marianne took out a stack of photos held together with a rubber band.

"I remember this," she said. "When Bill Clinton was in California, Papa insisted I drive him to National City. We waited in the sun for three hours. He refused to sit on the ground for fear he wouldn't be able to stand up again. I bought him a green hat."

We remembered the episode, but Marianne continued.

"Papa told Clinton he was ninety years old and had gotten his citizenship just in time to vote for him. The president shook his hand, thanked him, and moved on to touch other sweaty palms. A few feet away, he stopped, came back, looked Papa in the eye, and said, 'I am proud to meet you.' He then took out a tri-colored pen from his pocket and handed it to Papa. That's when I snapped the picture." Marianne shows us the glossy prints of the famous green hat.

I remembered being at my father's house when the photo department at Price Club called to ask if we really wanted forty-eight pictures of a blurry baseball cap. Papa had said, *Of course*. When he realized, however, that neither his face nor Bill Clinton's appeared, he decided not to include the prints in his Christmas cards.

Near midnight, we ripped open the dark lawn bag that contained Christmas wrapping papers. When Viv pulled out a nest of tinsel in her rubber-gloved hands, we froze with delight. Amidst the silvery mesh, the patriotic pen stood out proud and defiant. Sylvie extracted it and to our enormous relief, the string and the gold rings followed.

My father's ring was thick and well-rounded with my mother's name engraved on the inside. Mama's was a thin oval, the letters worn flat by years of worried fingering as she raised five children while Papa was in China, the Balkans and Africa on UN missions.

We hauled out multiple trash cans to the curb and closed the door on the over-crowded garage that contained furniture from France, African masks, boxes of books in Chinese, French and English, ivory carvings acquired before the ban on elephant tusks, letters, precious handmade gifts from children and grandkids, and other treasures accumulated throughout decades of married life.

By the time my sisters landed in Newark, the shiny sanitation truck had scooped up the cans and compressed their contents. Before leaving, my sisters had cleaned the rings and stored them, along with the Clinton pen, in a holiday gift box marked: *Papa's Rings. Do Not Throw Away.*

WIND ADVISORY

Like an ill-mannered guest
the wind moves on,

leaving behind a mess—
clusters of men, women,

confused children,
bewildered babies,

downed poles,
a battlefield of awnings,

the amputated limbs
of wounded trees,

cars crushed like soda cans,
also, an eighteen-wheeler on its side.

One man killed: steering column
sandwiched between airbag and ribcage.

The moon protests the violence
refuses to attend the night.

Big-mother clouds lumber six feet apart,
their pregnant bellies breaking water,

fire-hosing debris—yet, between mud
and grass, litters of yellow buttercups,

dandelion lashes surfing the wind.
The sun winks.

Far away, a hairline-fractured rainbow.
Still, a rainbow.

ACKNOWLEDGMENTS

I am profoundly grateful to my mother, Nicolette Laloy Hsu, who loved poetry and gave me my first book of poems on my sixth birthday. She also read to us constantly and gave me countless journals, which I filled with prose from the time I could write. I came to writing poetry much later in life when I signed up for a class with poet Steve Kowit at Southwestern Community College. The unexpected death of this gentle teacher deeply affected me and caused me to switch from nonfiction to poetry. Since then, several inspiring teachers and writers have encouraged me and offered valuable suggestions. Among them are Heather Eudy, Laure-Anne Bosselaar, Dan Veach, Sierra Nelson, Scott Bentley, Heal McKnight, Raina León, and Lee Herrick. I also wish to thank my fellow writers Yvonne Perry and Nancy Lemke. For weekly writing prompts "a la brava" and ongoing community, I thank poet and musician Francisco Bustos and the members of the Drum Circle. While I am not a lover of technology, I have to admit that many of these classes, writing groups and support systems were made possible by Zoom, which entered my life in the Covid-19 shutdown but has continued to serve me.

I am immensely grateful to Aaron Laughlin, Sarah Godlin, Noelle Doblado, and Kyle Morgan at The Press at Cal Poly Humboldt for their support in turning this manuscript into a book. And finally, this collection would not be possible without the ongoing editorial wisdom of my daughter Christina.

I gratefully acknowledge the editors of the following journals where versions of these poems previously appeared:

"Evaporation," *Atlanta Review*, Spring/Summer 2008; *Magee Park Poets Anthology,* 2009.

"Latin Mass," *Toyon Multilingual Literary Magazine,* volume 67, 2021; *Atlanta Review,* volume 23, Fall 2016.

"Wild Goose Pagoda," *Atlanta Review,* Fall/Winter 2010.

"Girl Child" (as "Second Child") and "Chinese Papers," *California Quarterly,* 2008.

"White Swan Hotel," *Magee Park Poets Anthology,* 2009.

"Why Professor Gao Sings," *Atlanta Review,* Fall/Winter 2009.

"Paris Morning," *A Year in Ink,* volume 6, 2013.

"Black Marker," *Bullets into Bells: Poets & Citizens Respond to Gun Violence,* September 9, 2022.

ABOUT THE AUTHOR

Claire Hsu Accomando was born in Switzerland to a Chinese father and French-Armenian mother. She spent her early childhood in rural France, separated from her father who was in China during WWII. Her memories of the war years are collected in her memoir, *Love and Rutabaga* (St. Martin's Press), released in a French translation in 2020 (L'Harmattan). Reunited after the war, the family moved to New York when her father joined the United Nations.

While Accomando graduated from NYU with a science degree, she was always drawn more to the arts. She taught History through Art and English as a Second Language in Southern California for many years. Her poetry has appeared in journals including *Atlanta Review, Mudfish, Toyon Multilingual Literary Magazine, Slab,* and *Bullets into Bells.* Her artwork has appeared in *Three Hearts: An Anthology of Cephalopod Poetry, Moon Water: An Anthology by Spell Jar Press,* and *JustArts: Call & Response.* She also has published nonfiction in *Ararat, Critical Flame, Women in World History, The Christian Science Monitor, Artweek,* and other publications.

Accomando lives in Bonita, California, and defines poetry as distillation: you start out with a truckload of potatoes and end up with a shot of vodka.

www.ingramcontent.com/pod-product-compliance
Lightning Source LLC
Chambersburg PA
CBHW051233120626
46547CB00013B/1624